THE COMFORT WOMEN

A HISTORY OF JAPANESE FORCED
PROSTITUTION DURING THE SECOND
WORLD WAR

WALLACE EDWARDS

Absolute Crime Press
ANAHEIM, CALIFORNIA

Contents

ABOUT ABSOLUTE CRIME

Absolute Crime publishes only the best true crime literature. Our focus is on the crimes that you've probably never heard of, but you are fascinated to read more about. With each engaging and gripping story, we try to let readers relive moments in history that some people have tried to forget.

Remember, our books are not meant for the faint at heart. We don't hold back--if a crime is bloody, we let the words splatter across the page so you can experience the crime in the most horrifying way!

If you enjoy this book, please visit our homepage (www.AbsoluteCrime.com) to see other books we offer; if you have any feedback, we'd love to hear from you!

PROLOGUE

During World War II as many as 200,000 women, commonly called comfort women, were forced into prostitution, brutally beaten and raped, and held prisoner throughout Asia under the direct control of the Japanese military. Comfort stations, or state-sanctioned, supported and operated brothels, existed in Japan, the Philippines, China, Indonesia, Hong Kong, Thailand, and elsewhere. By the early years of World War II, there were comfort stations and comfort women nearly everywhere there were Japanese troops, from major military posts to the battlefield. The comfort women confined and forced to work in these brothels came from Korea, Japan, Indonesia, China, the Philippines and the Netherlands.

The stories of the comfort women remained untold in much of the world through most of the 20th century, until the 1980 and 1990s when, with great courage, these now elderly Korean women began speaking out about their experiences during the war. Most had spent their lives keeping their experiences secret, sometimes even from their own families. Once a few came forward, many more were willing to share their own experiences, sometimes anonymously. The former comfort women from Asia and elsewhere shared their stories with the world, leading to a new recognition of their plight from the international community.

Beginning in the 1930s in China, Japan established widespread comfort stations or brothels for its officers and soldiers. These comfort stations were staffed by comfort women or juugun ianfu and were state-run, mandated and supported by the Japanese military. The military justified the existence of the comfort stations in a number of ways and eventually, at the end of the war, destroyed much of the evidence of their existence in an attempt to deny involvement in widespread sexual slavery. When the military and Japanese government acknowledged the existence of these comfort stations, for many years, they claimed the women were in the comfort stations voluntarily and were willing prostitutes, and that the comfort stations were privately managed, with little involvement from the Japanese government. Even today, some Japanese officials attempt to justify the existence and captivity of comfort women as a necessity.

While the euphemistic term comfort women sounds relatively innocuous, perhaps like it refers to prostitution, under no circumstances should this be viewed as a voluntary commercial enterprise, regardless of claims made by Japan in the past. Comfort stations bore no resemblance to a commercial brothel or voluntary prostitution. In some cases, these comfort stations have been called forced prostitution; however, this too is an inadequate term. The comfort women were deprived of their freedom, raped repeatedly, and treated as sexual slaves. Many, perhaps up to 75 percent, certainly died in captivity, either from disease, battlefield injuries or brutal treatment, while those who survived bore both physical and psychological scars that lasted throughout their lives.

The history of comfort stations and comfort women is a shameful one for Japan and one that remains largely unacknowledged. Until approximately 1991, Japan claimed all brothels during the war years were privately run and unaffiliated with the military. Only when undeniable documentary evidence was discovered did the Japanese government acknowledge and apologize for the actions against these women.

Organizations in Korea, the Philippines and the United States continue to fight for the rights of former comfort women to be recognized and compensated for their suffering during the war, as the number of surviving women declines with each year.

[1]

THE ESTABLISHMENT OF COMFORT STATIONS

By the early 20th century, Japan controlled a significant portion of Asia and had become a prominent military power in the region. Korea and Taiwan were both under Japanese control by the early 20th century, and both Koreans and Taiwanese were both, officially, considered Japanese; however, they were frequently treated as second-class citizens. Between 1910 and 1920, the Japanese military controlled Korea entirely. Extreme acts of violence occurred, frequently in response to any potential rebellion or attempts to preserve a Korean state; however, conditions improved somewhat in Korea after 1920. Successes in Taiwan and Korea led to a desire for additional land and power, even as Japan worked to build up Korea, creating urban centers and infrastructure. While Japan created much of the defining structure in Korea during this time, many of the people remained poor, rural and uneducated. Systems and services in Korea were set up to benefit Japanese residents, rather than Koreans.

Historically, the Japanese army had a somewhat good reputation with regards to the treatment of civilians. Invasions and occupations were generally conducted in a professional manner, with relatively little harm to civilians, including rape and murder. The Japanese army was reasonably well disciplined and many areas put up little if any resistance. This positive reputation changed from 1910 onward, both in China and elsewhere. As early as 1919, reports of atrocities in Korea, including murder and rape, reached Australian newspapers, particularly in response to resistance efforts. The treatment of Korean civilians during the period between 1910 and 1920 is reflected in their later exploitation as comfort women, some 80 percent of whom were Korean.

In 1927, the nationalist government established in China by Chiang Kai-Shek faced strong opposition from Mao Tse Tung's communist party. During the worldwide economic recession that began in 1928, Japanese trade exports to China dropped dramatically and anti-Japanese sentiment increased in China. By 1930, civil war had broken out between the communists and nationalists in China, weakening the state. The powerful Japanese army, against imperial orders, invaded and occupied Manchuria in 1931, in northeast China, taking advantage of the situation to gain access to the rich natural resources of China. The invasion of Manchuria marks the beginning of the Sino-Japanese War.

Having met little resistance, as the Chinese government was primarily concerned with their own internal disputes, the Japanese continued to encroach on Chinese territory. In 1932, the Japanese army advanced into the city of Shanghai. During the invasion of the city, large numbers of local women were raped by the invading forces, and many civilians were killed.

International residents in Shanghai remained relatively safe, as the civilians of China were at the greatest risk from Japanese troops entering the city. The traditional relatively humane treatment of civilian populations had come to an end for Japanese forces.

Following the invasion of Shanghai in 1932, Japanese Lieutenant-General Okamura Yasuji requested that comfort women be sent to Shanghai in an attempt to prevent the widespread rape of civilian women. This is the first incidence of state-sanctioned and sponsored comfort stations for the army, and was based on an already extant small-scale naval practice. Following Okamura Yasuji's request, Japanese brothels were set up in China by both the Japanese army and navy. In his 1970 memoirs, he recounted his own responsibility with regret.

Japan already had a long history of organized and regulated prostitution, including registration, health exams and active management, often by the military police, or kempeitai. In Korea, similar regulations were implemented after 1910, under the control of the kempeitai, but were less effective. The desire to implement a regulated system of prostitution was not a foreign concept within Japanese culture, and similar protocols were initially used in the military comfort stations. In this regard, the comfort stations developed out of an extant legal system. Historically and unsurprisingly, both in Asia and elsewhere, prostitution and the military have always been linked; however, it was, in most cases, a voluntary commercial arrangement.

During the early 1930s, the majority of comfort women were already prostitutes, recruited by the government, most often in the city of Nagasaki. Nagasaki had a large number of prostitutes and a substantial, in modern terms, red light district. Some of these women were Japanese, but others were Koreans already living and working in Japan. While these women were often from poor families and may have been sold into prostitution by their families, they volunteered to serve in the comfort stations in China and found these postings advantageous. The pay was quite good and conditions were considered acceptable. Recruiters often offered to pay off brothel owners or other debt, allowing women the potential of freedom following their time as a comfort woman. Additional comfort stations were established in northeast China during the early 1930s. Comfort stations continued to exist in Japanese-occupied China throughout the 1930s, but the ethnicities of the women working them changed following the invasion of Nanking.

While the incursions into China had, prior to 1937, been relatively small in the absence of a formal declaration of war, a large-scale military effort began in 1937, again in Shanghai. The Sino-Japanese war that began in 1931 intensified in Shanghai in August 1937. While the invasion in 1932 had led to significant casualties, the incidence of rape and murder increased dramatically during the 1937 invasion of the city. Following the retreat of Chinese forces, the city was undefended. Surviving civilians sought shelter in the international quarter, protected by Europeans living in the quarter. Those unable to find shelter were subject to rape, murder and sexual slavery. While comfort stations were in operation in China by this time, they did not alter the outcome for civilian residents.

As troops progressed across China, they looted, raped and murdered civilians throughout the country. In late 1937, Japanese forces reached the city of Nanking, the capital of China since 1928. Nanking's population had ballooned as refugees fled Japanese-occupied regions and the violence that accompanied Japanese troops. There were approximately 600,000 civilians in the city when the Chinese invaded on December 13, 1937. Defending Chinese troops initially fled and eventually surrendered to the Japanese. The 90,000 Chinese troops assigned to defend Nanking were the first killed in the city.

Over the next six weeks as many as 250,000 to 300,000 civilians, many of them women and children, were massacred in the city. Men were used for bayonet practice, disemboweled and buried alive. Rape was widespread, with between 20,000 and 80,000 women and girls of all ages raped and murdered after the rape. Women were raped not only by Japanese soldiers, but also by members of their own family, forced at gunpoint. Acts of extreme brutality and violence became entertainment during the six-week invasion, commonly called the Rape of Nanking. The events in Nanking led to a war crimes tribunal and several executions following World War II. While the Japanese government has refused to acknowledge the extent of the atrocities in Nanking during the war, more evidence has come to light in recent years, including an 1100-page diary kept by the head of the local Nazi party in which he recounts stopping rapes, sheltering Chinese in foxholes and tells of the atrocities he witnessed during the Rape of Nanking. A vocal minority in Japan continues to claim that all deaths in Nanking were military.

Even before the invasion of Nanking, on December 11, 1937, the Japanese government and military became increasingly concerned by the widespread rapes occurring in China. Rape decreased local cooperation and made it more difficult to effectively occupy the country. Fundamentally, rape was not good for public relations with the community, causing civilian resistance. Additional comfort stations were ordered with the intent of reducing the occurrence of rape in China. At least one Japanese medical official questioned the use of comfort women and alcohol for relaxation, suggesting limitations on alcohol, additional leave and other forms of recreation, but his suggestions were ignored and the comfort station system remained one of the few morale-boosters present for the Japanese troops.

Local women were recruited for the new comfort stations in China, particularly after the Rape of Nanking; however, there were concerns that they would not want to serve in the comfort stations, even when offered payment. While Japanese prostitutes were originally recruited to staff the comfort stations, the number of women needed and number of stations established led the military to attempt to recruit local women. Coercion or force may have been used to recruit women to the comfort stations, even during this early period in the history of the stations, but there is little documentary evidence from this period and few Chinese women have come forward to share their own experiences. Officials expressed in military letters and reports, from late 1937 on, that the women were "pushed hard" and shared that officers and high-ranking individuals also visited the comfort stations. Their concern with staffing suggests that these comfort stations were now far from the desirable option presented to Japanese prostitutes a few years earlier. It is unknown how many Chinese women were recruited, coerced or forced into the comfort stations in China and elsewhere.

By early 1938, it had become apparent to at least some in the Japanese military that employing local women as prostitutes was creating negative sentiment among the people of China, and again, presenting a potential challenge with local cooperation. Local women also posed a higher security risk, as their alliance was to the local military and community, rather than the Japanese or a foreign country outside of the region. Given these considerations, the military began to more actively import comfort women from out of the region, rather than employing locals in China. While a few of these women were Japanese, the majority were Korean, some, but not all, already residing in Japan. Around the same time the support among the military for the existence of comfort stations increased. Comfort stations were, according to military documents, established specifically to provide a sexual outlet for Japanese soldiers, in the mistaken belief that this would eliminate rape of local women by invading or occupying troops.

As of 1939, the Japanese army attempted to provide one comfort woman per 100 soldiers. This was a relatively low number, as there was later a goal of one woman per 35 soldiers. Surviving military documents refer to these women as "imported," much as rations and other goods were. In some wartime documents comfort women were categorized with "war supplies" on shipping invoices. Based on documentary evidence, it is likely that most comfort women in China in 1939 were Korean.

The comfort stations were regulated by the military to ensure the safety and well being of the soldiers and officers using the facilities. Measures were taken to reduce the spread of sexually transmitted diseases, including condoms and regular medical exams. Officially, the women were to receive food, shelter, clothing, medical care and wages for their services. While Japanese soldiers did pay a small amount to use the comfort stations, in many comfort stations throughout the Pacific the women were not paid at all and, in fact, the brothels provided a source of revenue for the military.

There were three types or categories of comfort stations. While the specific management of the comfort stations varied, all were under military control. In many cases, the comfort stations were largely controlled by the Japanese military police or the kempeitai, and these individuals were responsible for some of the most brutal atrocities of the war years, particularly acts of violence toward comfort women. While the army officially supervised the station, day-to-day management and conditions were, from 1938 onward, often in the hands of private operators, treated as paramilitary contractors. Some of these contractors were Japanese brothel owners, while others were retired military officers. Nearly all private brothel proprietors were Japanese. Since many stations were handled by private contractors, conditions varied from station to station.

The first type of comfort stations were permanent installations, located on military bases. While these were primarily staffed by Korean or Chinese women, some Japanese women also worked in these stations and served the officers on base.

These comfort stations were housed in permanent buildings and typically had scheduled medical examinations by military doctors. The women were often entitled to military rations or fed in the military mess hall.

Food and hygiene were adequate and a formal ticketing system was in place. These facilities were, on the whole, somewhat better managed, with access to medical treatment for sexually transmitted diseases, time off to recover from illness, and days off for menstruation.

A second type of comfort station was attached to large troop divisions and, in many cases, moved with the troops. Both permanent and large division comfort stations could be directly run by the military or by private proprietors under military supervision. Stations attached to large troop divisions were less well managed and were typically not staffed by Japanese women, but could request comfort women through the army supply system.

Many were staffed by Korean women, who were used by both officers and enlisted men. Conditions varied in these comfort stations, but were often less well regulated and harsher.

The third type of comfort station was located in the war zones or along battlefields. These were poorly supervised and were managed by individual battalions, rather than private proprietors.

While permanent and larger division comfort stations were under the control of military authorities and were staffed largely by Japanese or Korean women, local women were often coerced or forced into smaller battalion level comfort stations.

Some battalion level stations did receive shipments of women or visits from women from other comfort stations. As the comfort station system expanded during World War II, this basic three-part structure remained consistent throughout the Pacific.

[2]

REASONING AND JUSTIFICATION

While the comfort stations were originally established to prevent rape and maintain the cooperation of the local people under occupation, the military justifications for the comfort stations went well beyond relations with local people. As a tool for rape prevention, the stations failed in many ways. First and foremost, rapes do not occur because of sexual frustration or a lack of access to sexual activity. They are a crime of violence, unrelated to sexual desire. The rape of civilian women was not caused by sexual desire, but violence and dehumanization. The comfort stations did not reduce the prevalence of rape of civilians and, moreover, institutionalized rape as an accepted practice within the Japanese military. That continued, both in and out of the comfort stations, throughout the Pacific.

Sexually transmitted diseases were widespread and it was believed that creating a structured environment and controlling sexual activity would reduce the instance of disease among the troops. During the 1918 Chinese invasion of Siberia, as many as one in seven Japanese divisions were disabled by sexually transmitted diseases acquired through sexual contact with prostitutes in the community. In larger comfort stations, women received regular medical check-ups; however, access to medical care was minimal or unavailable in battlefield stations. In larger comfort stations, women were removed from service during treatment for sexually transmitted diseases. In smaller stations, women often received no medical treatment, and, according to the testimony of some former comfort women, were sometimes killed to prevent the spread of disease. No care was given to the women's health or well-being, simply to disease prevention.

Access to sexual activity was considered recreational or a morale booster, and believed to increase the fighting spirit among the troops. The Japanese army did not offer leave or other opportunities for recreation. Comfort stations were one of the few strategies implemented to relieve stress for the troops. Traditional Japanese superstitions suggested that sex might protect a soldier from injury on the battlefield and that going into battle without having had sex, or as a virgin, was bad luck. Even soldiers reluctant to use the comfort stations were often forced or cajoled into it.

The comfort women were controlled and contained, often not allowed to leave the comfort station or allowed to do so only under guard. Keeping women in a controlled environment and relying upon women who often had no ability to speak the language or defend themselves prevented any possibility of espionage or the exchange of secrets. In some comfort houses, women were assigned Japanese names and forbidden even to speak to one another. A desire to prevent possible espionage likely contributed to the use of Korean women throughout the Pacific. Koreans were subjects of the Japanese emperor and, by the time women were sent into the comfort stations, all Korean resistance efforts had been effectively eliminated. Koreans of both genders had, by World War II, become a slave labor force for the Japanese.

Finally, the military also relied upon the brothels as a source of income, providing the women with very little and taking in a substantial amount from the soldiers. Fees varied, depending upon the rank of the soldier or officer and race of the woman, but few women received what they were due. While early letters suggest that they intended to pay the women well, women working in the brothels were charged an exorbitant amount for their housing, medical exams, food and necessities. Even when paid for their service, they were not allowed to leave the comfort station and had no personal freedom. Regardless of payment, they were still held without the ability to leave, did not consent to the activity and should be viewed as sexual slaves.

[3]

RECRUITMENT

Just as there were three types of comfort stations, there were also three distinctly different means of bringing women into the comfort station system; recruitment, deception, and coercion or force. Recruitment was likely the least common method of these. Most women and their families, particularly in Korea, were deceived; however, a great many were coerced through violence or simply abducted. There is only minimal documentary evidence concerning recruitment or the role the Japanese government or military played in recruiting comfort women. Most of the evidence for the recruitment, particularly through deception or force, of comfort women comes from the women's own testimony and stories.

The first comfort women were recruited in Japan, typically in traditional centers of prostitution. Most were, likely, already professional prostitutes, while others were young women in need of work and were willing to consider prostituting themselves or were forced into it by their families. Many of these women were poor Koreans, already living and working in Japan. These were contractual arrangements, typically with an end date. At least one medical officer noted that the younger, Korean women were less likely to have sexually transmitted infections, as opposed to the older Japanese prostitutes.

Japanese brothel owners aided in these recruitment efforts, often serving as the primary recruiters. Japanese women who served in the comfort stations were largely older and, typically, already working prostitutes. These women typically served in the largest comfort stations, often providing not only sexual services, but also conversation to the officers. While Japanese officers often preferred the Japanese prostitutes, enlisted men report having found them condescending.

Deception was not involved in the early recruitment of Japanese women for the comfort stations, and working prostitutes were offered financial incentives to become comfort women. Even later in the comfort stations' history, a few Japanese women remained, typically in larger facilities.

Young Japanese women were not encouraged to serve in the comfort stations as they were potential mothers and wives of a new generation of Japanese soldiers. It was also assumed that Japanese soldiers would be more likely to think of their sisters, wives or neighbors serving and feel uncomfortable or lose trust in the army.

Initially, once the Japanese military chose to focus recruitment efforts in Japanese-controlled territories, particularly Korea, similar recruitment strategies were used. Women working as prostitutes or those willing to work as prostitutes were offered incentives to volunteer to serve as comfort women. They were, almost certainly, told that they would be well paid and that the comfort station would be a better opportunity, allowing them financial freedom following a term of service to repay debts incurred to the army or private brothel owner. As the war expanded, it became clear that the relatively small number of prostitutes available would not be adequate to serve the large number of troops in battle.

Most Korean comfort women were deceived into forced service in the Japanese comfort stations. Many of the recruiters were, themselves, Korean, and had little trouble gaining the trust of the women or their families. Young women were promised work in factories, nursing, or other professions in Japan. They were promised good pay and the ability to send money home, as well as opportunities for education. Recruiters offered cash bonuses to the impoverished families, further enticing young women to volunteer. The opportunity to help their families and earn an income was welcome.

Most of these young girls, typically between 14 and 18 years old, had no idea or expecta-

tion that their voluntary service involved prostitution, rather than factory work. Arrangements
were typically made quickly and within just
hours or days, young women were gathered
into transports and on their way to a comfort
station. The Japanese government provided
military-issued civilian travel papers or certifi-
cates of identification, allowing these women
to travel without passports or other documentation. These travel papers are one of the most
convincing pieces of evidence for consistent
military involvement in the comfort stations.

From 1942 onward, the Japanese used the
National Labour Service Association law to
conscript Koreans and others into forced labor
service. Comfort women were not the only
ones subject to the law, as Korean men were
also used for forced labor of all sorts. While not
formally intended to force sexual labor, many
women mobilized as part of the Women's Voluntary Service Corps found themselves in comfort stations, rather than factories. By 1943,
service was compulsory, rather than voluntary.
While women and their families were, officially,

expected to consent to service, this require-
ment was frequently overlooked or ignored.
Even when they consented, in many cases, the
women and their parents were illiterate and
unaware of what they were signing.

While many women were recruited through
deception and lies, others were forced or coerced into serving as comfort women. Coercion
and force were more common where local
women were used in the comfort stations, but
likely also occurred in other recruitment situations, including in Korea. At least one woman,
involved in the Korean resistance, reported that
she was kidnapped, taken to the police station
and raped. She regained consciousness in a Japanese brothel. Other former Korean comfort
women reported beatings, or threats to their
family if they did not appear for transport. The
kempeitai were frequently employed as a
threat by Korean recruiters, leaving the girls
without any choice. Those who tried to hide or
escape feared punishment for themselves and
their families.

In some cases, girls were taken from their families at gunpoint or the families threatened if the girl refused or attempted to fight back against her abductors. While the family may have agreed, the agreement came under intense coercion and threat. Officers or soldiers sometimes raped the girls in front of their families, devaluing them in a culture that valued chastity and silencing any possible refusals. Some girls witnessed their parents or families killed before they were taken. Other women and girls recount being kidnapped or abducted off the streets or a workplace and taken to a comfort station. In these instances, no pretense of agreement was in place. Women in the Philippines have described abductions like these. While most Korean girls, recruited through deception, were in their mid to late teens, girls abducted were as young as 11 or 12 years old, particularly in Indonesia and the Philippines.

Many of the women recruited or coerced into serving as comfort women were Asian, but some Dutch women, originally residing in the

Dutch East Indies, were also forced to serve as comfort women. The East Indies were home to a larger European population, including some working prostitutes of European origin. Dutch prostitutes were the first recruited for the comfort stations in Indonesia. Local Indonesian women and women of mixed Indonesian and European origin were recruited voluntarily or forced into the comfort stations. There were a relatively large number of comfort stations in Indonesia, requiring many women to staff them.

While some women, including Europeans, did volunteer for the comfort stations, others, including young wives, widows and young girls were forced into prostitution. These women were interned in camps under the Japanese occupation, not unlike prisoners of war. In need of more comfort women, particularly highly desirable and more expensive Europeans, camp officials lined up young women between the ages of 17 and 28 to choose possible comfort women. Conditions in the camps were poor and some women may have volunteered, hoping for better access to food and resources. Others sacrificed themselves in the hopes of sparing their young daughters and other younger women in the camp. Most were simply forced to become comfort women, or were unaware what was happening when they were moved into the comfort station. The women were forced to sign an agreement, written in Japanese, before they were transported to the comfort stations. Former Dutch comfort women report that they understood what was to happen only after they reached the comfort station.

At least one extant military document suggests that the Japanese army was aware that women were being rounded up or kidnapped and notes that the army should choose civilian recruiters with care, to avoid this sort of behavior. The Japanese Ministry of War recommends close cooperation between recruiters and local police or military police to prevent violence or kidnapping. While there is a desire for an organized and pragmatic approach to recruitment, this implies that deception was preferred over force or coercion. There is no direct condemnation of kidnapping, but there is concern for the reputation of the army, as has been noted in other aspects of the comfort women system.

[4]

STRUCTURE AND REGULATION

The comfort stations varied widely depending upon what was available in the local area. They could be large buildings with individual rooms or small cubicles separated by hanging mats to tents or other rough constructions. Most rooms or cubicles held a bed, cot or mat made of plant materials and washing facilities or disinfectant. A few women describe more comfortable quarters, with individual bathrooms and access to clean linens and double beds, while others lacked even a bed or bedding. Some women, particularly in rural outposts, were expected to cook, do laundry or other housekeeping during the day, servicing men at night. In some places, women served fewer men and, occasionally, left the comfort station to become an officer's mistress.

Whether the station was managed by the military or by a private contractor, the military controlled the rules and regulations at the comfort station. These were determined on an individual basis, and included fees for service, schedules, condom usage, and medical examinations. Fees varied from station to station. Lower-ranking men paid less than officers and the rates were often based upon the race of the women. Japanese and European women were substantially more expensive than Chinese or Korean women. In most cases, men lined up and paid for a ticket, allowing them between ten and 30 minutes with a comfort woman. They were given the ticket and a condom upon payment. While official regulations suggest a higher time allotment, surviving comfort women's accounts suggest that many men spent only a few minutes with them and that they were expected to serve far more men than a 30-minute window would allow each day. In many comfort stations, hours were set by rank, with soldiers allowed during the day and officers at night. Officers could stay the night for an extra fee. The women were allowed very little time for rest during the night.

The military was responsible for medical exams, whether the station was managed by the army or a private contractor. Medical exams were to be conducted weekly, preferably by a doctor or medic. The medical exams, when they occurred, typically provided the women with at least a half-day off work each week. In rural stations, the exam may have simply been external, checking for blistering or visible infection. Surviving reports indicate how many women were menstruating or infected with sexually transmitted diseases each week.

While rules existed, both for the management of the station and even for the well-being of the women, there is little evidence that these were regularly enforced. In some cases, as in surviving rules for a comfort station in Shanghai, regulations were intended to improve conditions for the women. Violence against the women was disallowed and each man had 40 minutes, reducing the total number served during a working shift substantially. Regulations in Manila, in the Philippines note that women were free to choose to stay at the end of their contract and that minors could not be employed in the comfort station. While comfort station operators were officially encouraged to comply with regulations, provide payment, adequate food and acceptable conditions, they often did not do so. Former comfort women report having served large numbers of men each day, having been taken into the comfort stations in their young teens, and receiving regular beatings if they displeased customers or the management.

The Treatment of Comfort Women

While experienced prostitutes may have transitioned to life as a comfort woman relatively easily, most of the girls and young women sent to the comfort stations were not prostitutes. Former prostitutes likely avoided some of the most traumatic experiences of comfort women. Many were quite young and nearly all were virgins when recruited, deceived or abducted to serve in the comfort stations. While each woman's experience was unique, their stories share some distinct similarities. The comfort women, typically called "Ps" by the Japanese soldiers, were forced into the war and suffered and bore the scars of the wartime years for the rest of their lives.

Treatment of women recruited for the comfort stations varied depending upon how they were recruited or coerced into service. The largest number of comfort women were Koreans, typically coerced or deceived by promises of the Voluntary Service Corps. The girls were typically transported in groups, ranging from just a few women to more than a hundred. They were moved from rural areas by bus or train, then placed on large ships, often military transport vessels, to go to their final destination. They were often from the same region and were, in some cases, provided with national costumes and cosmetics during their journey. Once the ship arrived, they could be moved to another comfort station or kept in the local area for some time before they were again moved to smaller local comfort stations. Young women who were abducted were often transported in much smaller groups and kept in a smaller geographical area.

Upon arriving at the comfort station, often one on a larger military base, the girls were raped, typically by an officer. Japanese superstition suggested that having sex with a virgin before a battle would provide the officer with protection against death or injury. In many cases, they were raped multiple times on the first night or a few nights in the station, sometimes at gunpoint, and most often by officers. The girls describe pain, bleeding and beatings, particularly if they fought back against the assault. At least some young women committed suicide following the initial rape, but many were kept under close guard or their families were threatened if they killed themselves. While not all women describe this initial process, many do, some quoting the officers as saying they needed to be "toughened up" for work in the comfort stations. There is no evidence that former prostitutes underwent this process. Documentary sources note that experienced Japanese prostitutes adjusted quickly, but young Korean girls required several months to accept their fate.

After an initial night of gang rape or days of repeated, violent rapes, they were forced to begin working as prostitutes in the comfort station. Private proprietors, often a couple, were to be called "mother" and "father". The girls were given Japanese names, and, in some cases, banned from speaking Korean or other native languages. They were, in some cases, taught how to service the men, encouraged not to pick favorites and instructed on how to treat men of different ages and ranks. Women were taught to douche after sexual encounters, but rarely had time to do so, often relying on nothing more than a quick external wash between customers.

Condoms prevented many pregnancies in the comfort stations; however, herbal contraceptives, abortifacents and sterilization surgeries were also used. While condom supplies were ample in many comfort stations, in others women reported having to wash and reuse condoms and noted that some men refused to wear them, or that officers wore them, but enlisted men did not. At least one comfort woman has shared that she told men she had an infection to encourage them to wear condoms. Some former comfort women, including Jan Ruff, a Dutch woman, report being given pills to cause an abortion. Others recount being forced to drink herbal drinks to prevent pregnancy.

Most former comfort women report that they were expected to serve 10 to 20 men each day; however, some report as many as 30 to 40 men, and in at least one report, up to 60 to 70 men. The numbers increased prior to significant battles. At least one comfort woman has reported significantly fewer men, servicing only five men a day. Comfort women were often sent along on supply runs, to service troops at the battlefield, or sent to the war front with a division of troops. Living circumstances were poor in this situation and they were expected to serve a very large number of men. Conditions differed depending upon the location, the number of comfort women available, and the management of the comfort station.

Beatings, particularly if they attempted to resist, were common and no serious attempt was made to protect the women. Women were also more likely to be beaten or brutalized during especially busy shifts, as they became exhausted or even fainted. Some women reminded the soldiers that they were all "children of the Emperor" in an attempt to avoid brutality. Former comfort women often report particularly harsh beatings in the first days and nights as a comfort woman.

In many cases, they were not allowed time to eat or wash during shifts when they were working, particularly if the lines were unusually long and the shift especially busy. While some women were allowed breaks, many were not. These long shifts and large numbers of men served also led to inaccurate counts and a lack of adequate payment. While the ticketing system, theoretically, provided women with an accurate count, the tickets were sometimes taken at the door, rather than by the women. Some women tracked clients by making marks on the wall or paper to maintain a more accurate count in the hopes of being paid correctly. Many comfort women were simply young, illiterate and frightened. These women were too traumatized to maintain a correct count of men and advocate for themselves with the proprietors.

While all comfort women lacked personal freedom or the ability to refuse sex, the specifics of their situation varied from station to station. Some women were allowed some amount of time off and were free, with permission, to leave the station for brief outings. Depending upon the facility, women could take walks or engage in other activities, play cards during quiet times or even had record players for music. Others were under constant guard and were unable to leave at all during their time of service. It seems likely that women who were present voluntarily, including the Japanese, had more freedom than those who were deceived or coerced. A few women were able to convince soldiers to pay off their debts or were able to work off their debt and gain their freedom; however, most remained in captivity throughout the war if they were unable to escape. Women who attempted to escape the comfort stations were tortured or killed.

In some stations, as regulations dictated, women were allowed time off for menstruation, as well as time off for medical care, including illness due to overwork. While they were responsible for some amount of their own medical expenses, if the owner was considered to have overworked them, leading to illness, their responsibility was less. They were also allowed time off to treat sexually transmitted diseases, but the quality of examinations and access to treatment depended upon the location. Medical treatment costs were typically added to their total debt, requiring a longer time of service. At military bases, examinations were performed by doctors and treatment was adequate, but in rural areas, folk remedies and herbal medicines were less effective. Records suggest that the prevalence of disease varied, from relatively low to quite high, depending on the station. Urinary tract infections were also common, with rest suggested to treat. In cases of severe illness, like a uterine prolapse, the women could be sent home. While treatment of illness appears to have been typical, some comfort women tell of others who were taken away and killed when they became ill or were left untreated to die.

Food rations varied from very minimal to adequate, depending on the comfort station. Some women describe receiving only a few rice balls, while others were fed regular meals, including rice, dried meats, chicken and eggs. In some cases, women had the freedom to purchase supplemental food with wages or tips or received gifts of food from men. In some stations, Korean women were able to buy the makings for kimchi and other local foods, drying chilies in the comfort station. Later in the war, food was scarcer, both for comfort women and the military in general.

All women were to receive payment, typically around 30 to 40 percent of the total earned; however, many did not. Fees were, in theory, set to allow repayment of debt to the brothel owner in a single year; however, this rarely occurred. As noted, many proprietors did not accurately track the number of tickets sold or clients serviced to reduce women's wages. The costs for medical treatment, food and clothing were high, limiting women's access to pay. Those that did receive payment often deposited their money into military accounts and were unable to access it after the war. Many comfort women report never having been paid at all.

[5]

COMFORT WOMEN'S STORIES

Since the 1970s and 1980s, former comfort women have come forward, sometimes using pseudonyms, to share their stories. While documentary evidence may be lacking, Japanese military officials have, on a number of occasions, corroborated the women's testimony. Lower level Japanese enlisted men and higher-ranking Japanese officials have also shared their own experiences with the comfort stations, supporting the women's stories and memories.

While most of the comfort women to come forward have been Korean, one Japanese woman, Suzoko Shirota, shared her story in a

little-known 1971 memoir before her death.
Sold to a brothel owner at 14 years old by her
father, Suzoko was eventually sent to a comfort
station in Taiwan as a young woman. She did
not choose to go, but was under the control of
the brothel owners, her body and freedom sold
from one to another. She was kept under close
guard and could not leave without special permission. As in brothels in Japan, she was held
to pay off a debt, including expenses for housing, transportation and food. Suzoko shared
her story publicly both in her memoir and on
Japanese radio, providing one of the first voic-
es for comfort women.

The stories of two Korean women exemplify
those of many other women. Both were young,
poor and lived in rural communities. While both
women survived, they sustained substantial
physical and psychological injuries and were
unable to have children. Their lives were fundamentally altered by their experiences during
the war.

Yo Bok Sil was 17 years old when she was
abducted by Japanese officials in 1938. There

was no attempt at deception or coercion. Her father attempted to intervene and was beaten. She was transported on a cargo train with many other young women and eventually lodged in a Chinese house with small cubicles curtained off by straw mats. Two of Bok Sil's group of fifteen killed themselves following the first night in the comfort station and their rapes. Bok Sil and the other women in this comfort station were forced to service thirty to forty men daily, near the war front. While stationed there, Bok Sil was injured by shrapnel. She was given several months to recover before she was forced to resume work. Yo Bok Sil was eventually able to escape the comfort station with help from a Korean interpreter.

Yi Sang Ok had already left home and was working as a housemaid when approached with an appealing job offer. She was fourteen when she boarded a ferry, having been told that she was to work in a scrubbing brush factory. The journey took more than a month in the lowest part of the ferry. Upon arriving at Palau Island, Yi Sang Ok was taken to a comfort station managed by a Japanese couple. She spent nine years in the comfort station and was beaten and stabbed with a bayonet during that time. She did not know how much the men paid for her services and was only paid a small amount each month. When heavy fighting began in Palau, she and the other women in her comfort station escaped into the jungles, surviving by foraging, and were eventually repatriated by the Americans.

Another Korean comfort woman, Yi Ok Bun's experience began when she was only 12 years old. From a well-off family, Ok Bun was lured and coerced away from her home. She did chores in a comfort house for a short time, before spending five years working in the home of a Japanese officer as a nanny and housemaid. At 18, she was taken to a comfort station, where she, somewhat unusually, saw men only on the weekends. She was assigned other tasks during the week. She could speak Japanese and was reserved for the officers. Her education provided her with better status in the comfort station. While other women in the station saw 20 to 30 men a day, Yo Ki Bun did not and maintained her health in captivity. Upon her return to Korea, Yi Ok Bun, also known as Yi Ki Bun, did not marry. She joined the 1991 lawsuit.

Like Yi Ok Bun, Kim Hak Sun was relatively well educated, having studied kisaeng, including singing, music, calligraphy and etiquette. On a visit to Beijing, Kim Hak Sun was separated from her foster father and taken to a Chinese house. As reported by other former comfort women, Kim Hak Sun was raped repeatedly and then placed into a comfort station. Along with three other Korean girls, Kim Hak Sun was expected to sing, dance and service a number of men. The comfort women were forced to watch Chinese individuals beheaded during their time as comfort women. The women in the comfort station were not paid, but only fed and clothed.

Jan Ruff was one of the Dutch women enslaved in the comfort stations. While the women who testified in the court martial did so anonymously, Ruff has come forward recently and told her story in some detail. Ruff first publicly shared her story in Tokyo in 1992. She has provided one of the most thorough accounts of her experience. In February 1944, Ruff was one of ten young women chosen from an internment camp in Indonesia. The girls were ordered to pack a bag of their belongings and were taken, along with six other young women, to Semarang. The twenty-year-old Ruff packed not only personal items, but also her Bible and crucifix. The following day they were told what was to happen in the comfort stations and their families, still in captivity in the internment camps, were threatened if they did not comply. Jan Ruff describes her first night of service as a comfort woman, sharing details about the multiple men who raped her. As a European, Ruff was intended to serve only officers at night; however, she was also raped during the day, and even by the medical officer who performed routine examinations. In an attempt to make herself less attractive, Ruff cut off all of her hair, but this did not improve the situation. During her captivity, Ruff became pregnant, but attempted to refuse the pills intended to cause an abortion. They were forced on her and she miscarried the pregnancy. Ruff estimates that she spent three months in the comfort station. She had, prior to her enslavement, hoped to become a nun and had taken her preliminary vows, but the church would not allow this after the time in the comfort station. She moved to Australia after the war, married, and after multiple miscarriages and corrective surgery, was able to bring a pregnancy to completion.

The experience of some Filipina comfort women differed somewhat. Most were not recruited in an organized way, but were abducted from the streets or their homes. Many were quite young, with one as young as ten and they were often held in garrison quarters. Others were held in customarily managed comfort stations. The first Filipina woman to step forward was Maria Rosa Luna Henson, commonly called Lola Rosa. Lola Rosa was, at only 14, captured and raped by three Japanese soldiers. She joined the guerilla movement after the rapes, but was abducted by Japanese soldiers in

1943. Lola Rosa describes being raped by 24 men on her first day in captivity. Kept in captivity with six other women, the women were not allowed to talk to one another. Lola Rosa was raped by 10 to 20 men daily. While the other women were allowed time off for menstruation, she had not yet reached puberty and was not. Lola Rosa remained in captivity for nine months, until rescued during a guerrilla raid.

Tomasa Salinog's story is similar to Lola Rosa's; however, her father was brutally murdered during her abduction. She was brought to a comfort station at only 13 years old, which she described as a two-story house. Her memories of the comfort station are less clear than those of some other former comfort women; however, this may be due to her young age. During her time in the comfort station, she was expected to service four men a day and do laundry. She escaped from the comfort station, but was taken captive by a Japanese officer and raped repeatedly in his home, by him and others.

While a number of Filipina and Korean women have come forward and several Dutch women testified, relatively few Chinese women have shared their experience. One former comfort woman of Chinese descent, known only as Madam X, was abducted in Malaya. Soldiers entered her home, injured her father and raped her in front of her family. She was taken from one comfort station to another, eventually servicing 10 to 20 men a day. She does not report being paid, but did receive adequate food and lived in a clean environment. While she describes a great deal of pain, she remembers a few of the men with some fondness, as they treated her kindly, bringing her food and gifts.

The Psychological and Cultural Context

While prostitution had always accompanied armies, the comfort stations and the experiences of the comfort women were very different from commercial prostitution or the experience of the camp follower. Camp followers or brothels serving the military were, traditionally, made up of women who were present voluntarily. While coercion was certainly present in some instances, it was not institutionalized, supported by the military and it did not occur on the scale it did during World War II.

Access to prostitutes had traditionally provided men with sexual release while in the army; however, in the west, men typically accessed these services on their time off or while on leave. Conditions in the Japanese army did not allow for any sort of leave time or time off. Furthermore, enlisted men in particular were very poorly treated in the Japanese army. Beatings were common for the slightest infractions, from a perceived insult to a superior officer to infractions in uniform care. Men were even beaten following inspections for sexually transmitted diseases. The brutality of the Japanese army likely contributed to the brutality with which the comfort women were treated. The men, particularly those with the least power, took out their own frustrations on the women available to them.

Some men expressed discomfort with the comfort stations, but many were pressured into the experience regardless. Even those who had little interest in the comfort women frequently expressed their discomfort with the situation in personal terms, rather than concern for the women's health, willingness or well-being. In recent years, some former Japanese soldiers have issued their own personal apologies for the harm done to comfort women.

Women of all different nationalities were forced to serve as comfort women, but nearly all were from cultures that placed a high value on female chastity. The women who psychologically fared best through this experience are those who were already prostitutes or were, at least, not young and inexperienced. These survivors found the experience, in the words of one Dutch comfort woman, "endurable" and suffered significantly less following the war; however, it seems likely these women were also in better living situations and more amply staffed and supplied comfort stations. While they were damaged by their experiences, they did not bear the significant burden of shame reported by younger women.

Korean culture, in particular, was based on Confucian belief systems. Confucianism not only placed duty to the family at the forefront of belief, but valued women's chastity, even over their lives. During historical invasions of Korea, women who committed suicide to avoid rape were particularly honored for their actions. Once a girl or woman had been raped, suicide was considered the only honorable alternative. To survive the experience left a woman with few options, as she could no longer be a wife and mother in Korean society. Rape and forced prostitution were not viewed as crimes against women, but rather against chastity. This belief made the women's situations even more psychologically challenging, as the brutality of their situation was accompanied by shame and feelings of worthlessness.

Outside of Japan, the girls and women chosen for the comfort stations were, primarily, young and inexperienced. They were typically poor and often illiterate. A lack of social standing, trauma, and lack of education combined to make this the most controllable population available for forced prostitution. Neither the women nor their families had the power to protest, even when they understood the situation. Desperation and ignorance made deception remarkably easy for recruiters.

As noted, racial considerations came into play in the comfort stations. Women of desirable races, including Japanese and Europeans, were more expensive, less common, and often reserved for wealthier and higher-status officers. The vast majority of comfort women were drawn from nationalities that the Japanese identified as second-class. While these women were primarily Korean, the same or worse treatment applied to women of other Asian countries.

[6]

THE END OF THE WAR

For those comfort women who survived the brutality of rape and the conditions in the comfort stations, the end of the war brought new dangers. Many comfort stations were located on the battlefield, placing the women in the line of fire. Some women escaped in the chaos at the end of the war, others were killed in battle or by Japanese troops. Those who survived often did not find their freedom at the end of World War II.

The women were no less busy as the end of the war approached. They occasionally had additional free time when large numbers were away, particularly if they were working at a permanent comfort station, but many saw larger numbers in the final months and weeks of the war. While kamikaze pilots, destined to die to complete their missions, were provided with free sex in their final week, other men at the front also relied heavily on the remaining comfort women, some visiting daily, out of superstition, desperation or even a frightened desire for human comfort and contact. Even with the realities of their own situation at hand, some of the women recount these visits with sympathy and compassion for the soon-to-die soldiers.

As allied troops advanced, Japanese forces had two honorable choices. They could fight to the death or they could commit suicide. Many chose suicide. The women accompanying divisions facing inevitable defeat were killed along with the men committing suicide. In at least one story, a Japanese prostitute asked the commanding officer to conduct a marriage ceremony with one of the soldiers to allow her to die a wife, rather than a prostitute. While some of the women took potassium cyanide, in other cases, soldiers were sent with machine guns to kill the comfort women and prevent their discovery. On Saipan in the Marianas, both com-

fort women and the civilian women of the population drowned themselves to avoid capture.

Women on the battlefield not only continued to provide sexual services, but were also
expected to serve as nurses, to help carry rations and other goods. In some areas, comfort
women retreated along with troops. They suffered the same struggles, including injury and
starvation, as the retreating soldiers. Many
comfort women were simply abandoned as the
troops moved on or were encouraged to flee
by the retreating forces. Some awaited rescue,
while others gathered their possessions and attempted to return home on their own. Those
who had been paid carried their money with
them; however, this military currency would
soon be totally value-less. The Japanese, even
at this early stage, expressed concern about
the discovery of comfort women.

Attempts at concealment began as the war
ended, with some women rapidly assigned
nursing positions, particularly Japanese women
and possibly colonial subjects, including Koreans. Nursing positions may have provided the

women with some degree of protection, as well as reducing awareness of the institutionalized forced prostitution throughout Asia under Japanese rule. Along with the attempt to dissolve the comfort stations, Japanese officials began destroying documentary evidence of the comfort stations and other wartime atrocities.

Comfort Women and the Occupying Forces

Even before the victory over the Japanese in August 1945, allied officials were aware of the existence of comfort stations and comfort women. Some Korean women in Burma were interrogated by a U.S. Psychological Warfare Team in August 1944; however, relatively few records of the minimal interrogation were kept. They did note that the women were not there willingly and had been forced into prostitution, but the primary interest of the United States at that time was the psychology of Japanese troops and the impact of the comfort stations on that psychology. A February 1945 report called Amenities in the Japanese Armed Forces described Japanese military brothels in some detail, including their existence, regulation and management. This information came from captured Japanese military documents. Interrogations of Japanese prisoners of war also produced evidence of the comfort stations during the war, including the varied nationalities of the comfort women.

Following the allied victory, American and other allied forces were, doubtlessly, aware of the existence of comfort women. Across the Pacific front, allied troops found groups of comfort women, sometimes disguised as nurses or Red Cross workers. While many photos of comfort women were taken by the allied troops, very few women were questioned or interrogated about their experiences. Allied forces repatriated some women to their home countries, including around 150 Korean women found in Okinawa, but largely ignored the issue of comfort women, either on a personal basis or as a crime against humanity. There was no intention or expectation that these women's experiences would be part of the war crimes trials to follow.

While most former comfort women were largely ignored, one group merited attention following the end of the war. In the Dutch East Indies, some of the comfort women were Dutch, rather than Indonesian. Approximately 200 to 300 Dutch women were working in Japanese comfort stations, at least 65 who had been forced into prostitution. These Dutch women were taken from the civilian internment camps; however, some women volunteered in the hopes of protecting younger women. The number forced into prostitution may, therefore, have been substantially higher than the Dutch court record indicates. The Dutch government sought justice for these women, notably the only non-Asian women among the comfort women. The Batavia Temporary Court Martial in February 1948 tried 13 Japanese military officials. One was sentenced to death and 11 others to prison terms. All convictions related to a single incident in the internment camps, as attempts to prosecute for a second incident in which women were sent from the internment camps to a comfort station ended in acquittal.

Several factors contributed to this widespread willingness to disregard this issue among the Allied forces. First and foremost, the majority of comfort women were Asian. Anti-Asian propaganda and sentiment among the allied forces likely helped to identify these women as part of the enemy force, rather than victims of the enemy. Even the Dutch, who did prosecute the Japanese for their use of Dutch women in the comfort stations, took no interest in the exploitation of Indonesian women or women of mixed heritage in the same comfort stations. Second, the Allied forces shared, in some ways, the Japanese attitude toward women and prostitution. It was widely believed that men, particularly at the front, had a right to sexual services. Finally, the Tokyo War Crimes Tribunal following the Second World War was specifically targeted toward offences against the Allies, rather than other Asian populations. The final peace treaty with the Allies, the San Francisco Peace Treaty, provided the

Japanese with some protection against further prosecution for war crimes. Since the majority of comfort women were Asian, rather than from Allied countries, this excluded them from any sort of justice during the post-war trials.

The Japanese government maintained the military structure of the comfort women system, now for the benefit of occupying Allied forces. In at least one instance, Japanese officials entertained American officers with Korean comfort women following the surrender. While some former comfort women worked in these comfort stations created for the occupying Allied forces, many of the women recruited after the end of the war were Japanese. These young women, frequently former factory workers, were told they were required for special voluntary service. While their service may have been, in name, voluntary, they had little real choice in the situation. In the economically devastated country, intimidation and coercion were not required to recruit women for the comfort stations; however, their service in these stations was no more consensual than that of other comfort women.

Under the supervision of Japanese guards, American soldiers visited comfort women in stations in Japan. Women who attempted to leave were stopped by the guards and were held captive in the comfort stations. Rape was, as it had been in occupied lands under Japanese control, a problem in Japan after the war, and again, the Japanese hoped that comfort stations would reduce the risk of rape among Japanese women. The women working in the comfort stations after the war were told that their service helped to protect other Japanese women from rape and dishonor While the comfort stations were much like those managed before the end of the war, there was no way to enforce condom use and prevent sexually transmitted diseases. Rates of sexually transmitted disease among the American troops soared and American military authorities banned the comfort stations not long after the end of the war.

[7]

SURVIVAL

It is not known how many women did not survive their years in captivity as comfort women. Some estimates suggest that as many as 75 percent of the 100,000 to 200,000 young women working as comfort women died during the course of the war. Brutality, murder, starvation, and conditions of war all contributed to deaths among the women, as did the potential for disease, both sexually transmitted and otherwise. Those that lived did not return to their former lives easily, even if they were repatriated by the Allied forces or their own efforts.

The physical toll of the experience was substantial for women who survived. Many women suffered from a variety of health problems, frequently caused by sexually transmitted diseases or attempts at treating those diseases. Sterility was very common, and few former comfort women were able to have families after the war. Some had been chemically or surgically sterilized, while others had sustained physical injuries or sexually transmitted diseases that prevented pregnancy. Many women had lasting injuries from beatings, torture or stab wounds, while some were injured during bombings or mortar attacks in the war.

Women who returned home frequently kept their experience a secret, telling only a few or no one at all. Many women claimed that they had, as promised, done factory work during the war years. Some of the former comfort women tried, valiantly, to return to their lives. A few women were able to marry and begin families on their own or through adoption. Even those women who did marry and were able to have children often retained significant psychological scars. They experienced a variety of psychological symptoms, many associated with what we would today identify as post-traumatic stress disorder. These former comfort women report a fear or hatred of men and trauma associated with sexual activity throughout their lives.

Some women, already married when forced into the comfort stations, were rejected by their husbands when they returned, on grounds of adultery or fear of disease. Many comfort women were unwilling or unable to marry, given the high status placed on virginity in Asian culture. Without the benefit of marriage, women in Asian society were outsiders, often impoverished and unable to make an independent life outside of sex work. Given that most of the women were from poor, rural communities, there was little government interest in their fate or in gaining any sort of reparations for their suffering.

Many former comfort women continued as prostitutes or worked in areas closely linked to prostitution, including singing and dancing for the benefit of occupying troops in Asia. While still working as prostitutes, the women had, in many cases, regained their physical freedom and some degree of choice outside of the comfort stations. Some comfort women had assimilated to their environment and did not attempt to repatriate to their home country. Years later, visiting Japanese in locations throughout Asia noted that some women in the community spoke Japanese and had had contact with the Japanese military during the war.

Diplomacy and the Comfort Women

The Allies were far from the only ones to ignore the issue of comfort women and the comfort stations prior to and during World War II. The women's home countries ignored the fate and future possibilities of these women, even when they were aware of what had happened. As young women had married or otherwise attempted to escape the Voluntary Service Corps, there is no doubt, that as time went on, the Korean population understood exactly what sort of labor was in store for the women. Many people knew what had happened to the comfort women. Both men and women felt substantial shame about what had occurred and avoided mentioning the subject. Some women who had done factory work during the war under the guise of the Women's Voluntary Service Corps avoided mentioning their own experiences to prevent any association with comfort women or forced prostitution. The comfort women themselves lived out their lives in secrecy, often lying to hide their experiences, even as they aged.

In 1951, Korea and Japan began talks to establish diplomatic relations between the two countries. The final Treaty on Basic Relations between Japan and the Republic of Korea was signed in 1965 and included significant financial reparations for Korea. These funds were used for economic development and social infrastructure within Korea, rather than for individual compensation for forced labor during the war years. Papers released in the 1990s suggest that Japan offered individual compensation at this time, but Korea opted for a lump sum grant to the government. Some 364 million dollars was provided to compensate individuals for forced labor during the colonial period and an additional 800 million dollars for damage done by colonial rule; however, Korea was free to disburse funds as desired. Since 1965, Japan has claimed that this government settlement eliminated any future responsibility to forced laborers, including comfort women. The issue of comfort women was not, specifically, mentioned at any point in these negotiations.

Speaking Out

What few discussions there were about the comfort women prior to the 1980s were primarily in Japanese and were not translated or widely circulated. These texts, including the autobiography of one Japanese comfort woman and Senda Kako's Military Comfort Women, were primarily read by academics. Kim Il Myon published The Emperor's Forces and Korean Comfort Women in the late 1970s. This was followed by a 1979 film, An Old Lady in Okinawa: Testimony of Military Comfort Woman. In 1982, a small group of academics and intellectuals actively spoke out against the Japanese policy of denial and misinformation with regard to Japanese actions as a colonial power and during the war, including comfort women. In 1993, Yoshida Seiji, author of the 1932 request for comfort women and comfort stations in Shanghai, wrote an account of his own activities during the war, including the forced draft of comfort women. While these works provided evidence about the comfort women system, it was rarely publicly discussed in Korea or Japan.

Conditions in Korea began to change in the 1980s, with the introduction of a new women's movement and new interest in women's rights and history. Prior to the 1980s, Korean economic policies were distinctly damaging to women. These policies exploited inexpensive female labor and helped to support a thriving sex trade, both in nightclubs and near American military bases. During the 1970s, women began to join together to gain the right to a subsistence wage and form labor organizations. The women's movement in South Korea grew substantially through the 1980s, beginning, for the first time, to challenge the traditional patriarchal culture of Korea.

Women's groups were the first to raise the issue of comfort women, called Chongsindae in some documents, both publicly and to the Korean government. At the 1988 International Conference on Women and Tourism, Yun Chung-Ok presented research into the Chongsindae. Her research and presentation connected the comfort women with the modern Korean sex trade. In 1989, women's groups staged a protest against a planned Korean emissary to the funeral of the Japanese Emperor Hirohito and drafted a letter to the government protesting the disregard for the comfort women. They were initially ignored by the Korean government. The Korean government claimed a lack of documentary evidence, and noted that further reparations were not possible under the terms of the 1965 agreement with Japan.

A planned state visit by the Korean president to Japan in 1990 provided a new opportunity for women's groups to bring up the issue of the comfort women and reparations for their suffering. Women's groups issued a list of demands prior to President Roh Tae Woo's visit to Japan, including an investigation into the comfort stations and an apology for the exploitation of the comfort women.

During the May 1990 visit, Japanese Emperor Akihito expressed regret for any sufferings caused by the colonial rule of Korea; however, in June a Japanese politician, Motooka Shoji, called for an investigation into the issue of comfort women. By June 1990, Motooka already had access to a great deal of documentary evidence, including a number of reports from the war zones that described regulations associated with comfort stations. While Motooka and others had seen evidence of the government involvement in the comfort women system, the government continued to deny all responsibility. The Korean women's groups responded to the government denial by providing documentary evidence supporting their claims, including the testimony of former comfort women and an official who drafted women into the Voluntary Service Corps.

Korean women's organizations continued to pressure Japanese and Korean officials throughout 1990, and the first organization designed specifically to advocate for comfort women was established in November of that year. This organization served to unite diverse women's groups to work together for the preservation of these women's stories and their financial needs in the present. The demands of the comfort women, as shared by a group of 37 women's organizations under the heading of the Korean Council on the Matter of Comfort Women, include not only financial reparations, but also an official acknowledgement and apology, full disclosure of all historical information, construction of a memorial or monument, and the correction of Japanese textbooks to include the truth about comfort stations in World War II. These demands were presented to the Japanese government. The government response continued to be one of total denial.

While Korean women's groups had begun to investigate and organize around the issue of Korean comfort women before and during

World War II, few former comfort women had come forward to share their experiences or been willing to go public with them. In 1991, Kim Hak-Sun, a widow without children or other family, shared her own testimony about her time as a comfort woman. In December 1991, Kim Hak-Sun filed suit against the Japanese government. During the early 1990s, several other former comfort women also sued Japan. Their case was based on international customary law, specifically allegations of crimes against humanity, as well as Japan's unconditional surrender. A number of women testified, some using pseudonyms and hiding their faces to protect their privacy. During the trial, the Japanese government admitted to the supervision and medical hygiene at the comfort stations, but nothing more.

Later suits, including lawsuits filed by Filipina, Dutch, Taiwanese and Malaysian comfort women followed. Filipina and Dutch women, perhaps because of the surrounding culture, have been more willing to speak about the comfort stations. Influenced by European culture, these women may have been less shamed by their experiences than Korean women. The Dutch women victimized during the war were the only ones to achieve any sort of justice, likely helping to provide a sense of closure. During the trials and later efforts to locate former comfort women, no Indonesian or Japanese women came forward to share their own experiences. The movement to provide restitution to comfort women was, largely, a nationalistic one. This may have silenced surviving Japanese women, or perhaps, since many Japanese comfort women were there by choice, they have chosen to keep their pasts private. While all of these suits reached the Japanese supreme court, appeals were not successful.

Both the Korean and Japanese government had alleged that there was no documentary proof of the women's accusations, prior to the trial. In 1992, in response to the comfort women's suit, a Japanese professor, Yoshiaki Yoshimi, began his own investigation into Japanese claims that military brothels had been an entirely private enterprise. In the records of the Japanese Defense Agency, dating to the 1930s, Yoshimi found substantial documentation to prove military and government involvement in the recruitment and enslavement of comfort women. He released his documentation to the press.

Following Yoshimi's 1992 discoveries and the publication of excerpts of these texts, as well as the discovery of other documentary evidence, the Japanese government issued a statement accepting responsibility for the comfort stations and the comfort women in 1993. Japanese textbooks were, at this time, altered to include a discussion of the comfort women. Hotlines and Victim Report Centers were set up in Korea and elsewhere, including Japan, to allow former comfort women and others familiar with the system to come forward and share their stories. Many in the public, including many in Japan, favored reparations for the comfort women. Japan, South Korea and North Korea each produced reports enumerating the evidence regarding comfort women; however,

Japan continued to, as much as possible, deny involvement in the recruitment of comfort women.

Comfort women testified before the United Nations in August 1992, sharing their stories and gaining significant international support. Following their testimony, the United Nations' Human Rights Commission officially identified the military comfort women system as a "crime against humanity". The United Nations recommended full disclosure, a full apology and financial compensation for the victims in reports in 1996 and after. The United Nations has identified the military comfort women system as sexual slavery, in violation of international laws.

In August 1993, faced with growing evidence, the Japanese government acknowledged that the military had not only provided supervision and medical support for the comfort stations, but also had been involved in the recruitment and coercion of women in Korea and elsewhere. An apology for the mental and physical harm suffered by the comfort women followed; however, the government did not claim legal responsibility. While many expected compensation to follow, there were strong right-wing elements in Japanese politics objecting to not only reparations, but even the acknowledgement and apology.

Rather than providing direct financial compensation to the women harmed, the Japanese government created a fund, the Asian Women's Fund, supported by private donations rather than the public monies. The fund was established in 1995 as a means of expressing regret and providing an organization to address other concerns related to comfort women's issues and history. The fund provided private compensatory payments of around U.S. $18,000 and medical welfare payments to some former comfort women. Additional funds were provided for nursing facilities and homes and other social welfare programs aimed at the well-being of women in Asia. A digital museum was created to preserve the history of comfort women and a five-volume compilation of documents relating to comfort women was released online and in print. The closure of the

Asian Women's Fund was announced in 2005, with the completion of a social welfare project in Indonesia and occurred in 2007.

A Korean fund raising effort in December 1992 provided former comfort women with a one-time payment and a small monthly pension. Additional fund raising has provided further funds for these women, in exchange for refusing payments from the Asian Women's Fund. Korean women's organizations strongly discouraged women from accepting these funds in lieu of proper government reparations. The creation of a private fund or organization allowed the Japanese government to avoid accepting legal responsibility for the comfort women program, claiming only a moral responsibility. This entirely avoided the issue of whether or not the comfort women system was a crime against humanity or a war crime.

The controversy continued throughout the first decade of the 21st century. Right wing elements in Japanese politics, including Shinzo Abe, who in 1993 objected to the apology, gained power. Abe was elected prime minister in 2006, leading a largely right-wing government and actively seeking the restoration of a more powerful and more traditional Japan. Shortly after his election, Shinzo Abe, along with a number of other members of the right-wing Liberal Democratic Party, denied the charges of coercion, claiming a lack of evidence. Abe's desire to revoke or alter the 1993 acknowledgement and apology led to substantial criticism from women's groups and the international community. Shinzo Abe served as prime minister in 2006 and 2007, but his opposition to the acceptance of responsibility for the comfort stations continued after his tenure as prime minister. As a member of the minority party in 2012, Abe signed a published declaration denying coercion and responsibility for the atrocities of the comfort women system. Abe's party gained the majority again in 2012, but the Japanese government nonetheless reaffirmed its 1993 apology in May 2013.

Not long after the government issued a statement in support of the apology, the mayor of the city of Osaka, Toru Hashimoto, publicly stated that comfort women were "necessary" during the war. Hashimoto went on to suggest that Japan had been singled out, since other nations also allowed brothels near military posts and even encouraged American troops to frequent sex workers in Okinawa. His remarks were met with intense international criticism in Asia and the United States. While Hashimoto did withdraw his comments about American troops currently in Okinawa, he continues to defend his statement that the comfort women were necessary. In response, two Korean former comfort women, previously scheduled to meet with Hashimoto, cancelled their visit.

EPILOGUE

The remaining few comfort women are now reaching the ends of their lives. Efforts by Korean women's organizations and others have provided them with some amount of financial security; however, they have not fully met their goals of reparation, acknowledgement and apology.

The apologies provided by the Japanese still ring untrue and inadequate to many, leaving these battle wounds raw and open. Growing movements in Japan, as reflected by the words of Toru Hashimoto, suggest that the gains made by the comfort women and their supporters may be tenuous at best.

BIBLIOGRAPHY

Asian Women's Fund, "The "Comfort Women" Issue and the Asian Women's Fund." Tokyo: Asian Women's Fund, 2004. http://www.awf.or.jp/pdf/0170.pdf (accessed on June 21, 2013).

Boling, David. Mass Rape, Enforced Prostitution, and the Japanese Imperial Army: Japan Eschews International Legal Responsibility? Baltimore: University of Maryland School of Law, 1995.

Chang, Iris. The Rape of Nanking: The Forgotten Holocaust of World War II. New York: Basic Books, 2012.

Chou, Chih-Chieh. "An Emerging Transnational Movement in Women's Human Rights: Campaign of Nongovernmental Organizations on

"Comfort Women" Issue in East Asia." Journal of Economic & Social Research 5, no. 1 (2003): 153-181.

Coomeraswamy Report to the United Nations. "Report of the Special Rapporteur on violence against women, its causes and consequences, Ms. Radhika Coomaraswamv, in accordance with Commission on Human Rights resolution 1994/45 Report on the mission to the Democratic People's Republic of Korea, the Republic of Korea and Japan on the issue of military sexual slavery in wartime." January 4, 1996. http://www.comfort-women.org/coomaras.htm (accessed on June 20, 2013).

Davidson, Amy. "The Mayor and the Comfort Women." The New Yorker. (May 20, 2013). http://www.newyorker.com/online/blogs/closeread/2013/05/the-mayor-and-the-comfort-women.html (accessed on June 21, 2013).

Hicks, George. The Comfort Women: Japan's Brutal Regime of Enforced Prostitution in the

Second World War. New York: W.W. Norton & Company, 1994.

Min, Pyong Gap. "Korean 'Comfort Women': The Intersection of Colonial Power, Gender, and Class." Gender and Society 17, no. 6 (December 2003): 938-957.

Soh, C. Sarah. "Japan's Responsibility toward Comfort Women Survivors." Japan Policy Research Institute Working Paper 77 (May 2001). http://www.jpri.org/publications/workingpapers/wp77.html (accessed on June 20, 2013)

Tanaka, Yuki. Japan's Comfort Women: Sexual Slavery and Prostitution during World War II and the U.S. Occupation. London: Routledge, 2002.

Yoshimi, Yoshiaki. Comfort Women: Sexual Slavery in the Japanese Military during World War II. New York: Columbia University Press, 2000.